CONTRARY CREATURES

Unique Animal Opposites

For Jen Hale

Copyright © 2018 James Weinberg

First published in 2018 by Page Street Kids,
an imprint of
Page Street Publishing Co.
27 Congress Street, Suite 105
Salem, MA 01970
www.pagestreetpublishing.com

Distributed by Macmillan, sales in Canada by The Canadian Manda Group

18 19 20 21 22 CCO 5 4 3 2 1

ISBN-13: 978-1-62414-580-3
ISBN-10: 1-624-14580-9

CIP data for this book is available from the Library of Congress.

This book was typeset in PMN Caecilia.
The illustrations were done digitally.

Printed and bound in China

Page Street Publishing uses only materials from suppliers who are committed to
responsible and sustainable forest management.

Page Street Publishing protects our planet by donating to nonprofits like
The Trustees, which focuses on local land conservation.

trustees

CONTRARY CREATURES

Unique Animal Opposites

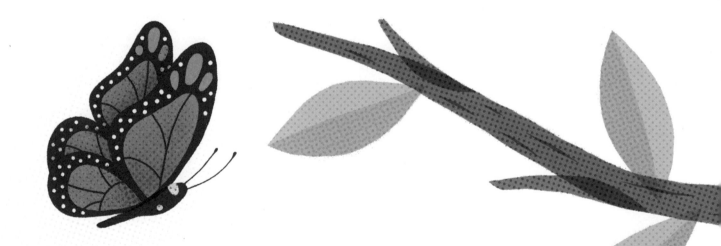

James Weinberg

PAGE
STREET
KiDS

Look closely!

Some animals blend
into the background,

while others want to
be seen by all.

Some animals live
in the hot desert,

while others are
happy in the cold.

Some move very slowly . . .

but some are fast.

Some animals eat plants.

And some plants eat animals!

Look up!

Some animals
fly high in the sky,

while others
swim deep
in the ocean.

Some animals like
to be clean,

while others
bathe in the mud.

Some are tiny . . .

but some are huge!

And some animals
lived long ago.

Look around!

Some animals
exist only in stories
and legends,

while others are real

but seem make-believe.

Some animals stay close to home,

while others migrate a long way.

Some like to be up early . . .

but some
stay awake
all night.

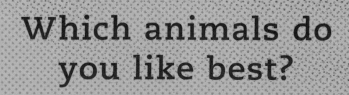

Which animals do you like best?

Curious about contrary creatures?

 CHAMELEONS change colors to cool down and warm up or to communicate with other chameleons. Also look in the art for a katydid.

 PEACOCKS refer to male peafowl. Females are called peahens. Peacocks use their bright feathers for courtship and mating rituals.

 GILA MONSTERS are native to the United States and live in the rocky deserts of the Southwest. Also look in the art for a scorpion and a gilded flicker.

 EMPEROR PENGUINS live only in Antarctica, and their feathers help keep them warm. Also look in the art for a polar bear and Antarctic seals.

 TORTOISES move slower than 1 mile per hour on land and can live to be between 80 and 150 years old. Also look in the art for a snail.

 HUMMINGBIRDS beat their wings anywhere from 720 to 5,400 times per minute, and they can fly between 30 and 60 miles per hour.

 OKAPIS, or forest giraffes, feast on the leaves, seeds, and fruit of more than 100 different plant species in the Central African rain forests where they live.

 VENUS FLYTRAPS are carnivorous, which means they eat meat—insects such as ants, flies, and beetles, to be exact.

 BALD EAGLES have extremely good eyesight and soar on a wingspan of 6 to 8 feet.

 DEEP-SEA DRAGONFISH live around 5,000 feet below the ocean's surface, deeper than sunlight can reach. Also look in the art for a cosmic jellyfish.

 SNOW MONKEYS, or Japanese macaques, like to spend time in hot springs and sometimes wash their food before eating it.

 HIPPOPOTAMUSES (HIPPOS), native to Africa, cover themselves in mud to get rid of insects, protect against sun damage, and keep cool.

 LADYBUGS are actually beetles and are less than half an inch long. Their bright colors and spots scare off predators.

 BLUE WHALES, the largest animal on Earth, can grow to be 100 feet long and weigh up to 200 tons. Also look in the art for krill.

 DINOSAURS are extinct reptiles that lived more than 200 million years ago. Look in the art for a Tyrannosaurus rex, a Dimetrodon, and a pterodactyl.

 WINGED UNICORNS are mythical creatures whose horns have magical healing abilities. Also look in the art for a jackalope, the Loch Ness monster, and a yeti.

 LEAFY SEA DRAGONS are related to seahorses and live off the western and southern coasts of Australia, where their appearance helps camouflage them.

 PANGOLINS are covered with hard scales and curl up into a tight ball when they feel threatened. Also look in the art for ants.

 SLOTHS live in trees and come down to the ground once a week. They travel an average of only 40 yards in a day.

 MONARCH BUTTERFLIES migrate 2,000 to 3,000 miles each year and inexplicably know the migratory route that's traveled only once in a butterfly's life span.

 ROOSTERS don't need light to know when it's a new day. They follow their internal "clock"—or circadian rhythm—when first crowing each morning.

 GREAT HORNED OWLS, are nocturnal—asleep during the day, awake at night. They have extremely good vision and hearing. Also look in the art for brown bats and fireflies.